■ PICTURE ■
WORD BOOK

The images on the cover of this book focus on toys that come alive in children's imaginations—just as words come alive when the magic of reading takes place.

MACMILLAN/McGRAW-HILL

Macmillan/McGraw-Hill School Publishing Company
New York   Chicago   Columbus

Editorial Staff

Editor in Chief	Judith S. Levey
Managing Editor	Helen Margaret Chumbley
Editors	Deirdre Dempsey, Susan R. Norton
Production Manager	Karen L. Tates

Art Staff

Design Director	Zelda Haber
Associate Design Director	Joan Gampert
Art Director	Murray Belsky
Design	Anna Sabin
Artists	Barbara Bash, Karen Baumann, Courtney Studio, Norman Dane, Nancy Didion, Dora Leder, Susan Lexa, Frederick Marvin
Clerical Assistant	David Salinas
Cover Art	Fred Winkowski

Macmillan/McGraw-Hill School Division
866 Third Avenue
New York, New York 10022

Printed in the United States of America

This dictionary is also published in a trade edition under the title *Macmillan Picture Wordbook*.

ISBN 0-02-195001-6/K-1

9 8 7 6 5 4 3 2 1

A Word To Parents And Teachers About The

Macmillan/McGraw-Hill Picture Word Book

A child's world is filled with spoken and written words. Words in the natural environment such as *Stop, No Parking,* and *Exit* cause children to become aware of the meaning of written language at an early age.

A picture word book extends children's knowledge of language by showing them that words name objects in not only their own environment but also in the larger world.

- When opening the *Macmillan/McGraw-Hill Picture Word Book* for the first time, children will probably want to flip through all the pages, stopping when something special catches their eye. Point out some of the words they may be interested in.

- Listening and talking together while looking at the *Picture Word Book* is important. There are recurring figures of children in the book. Invite children to find these children in several scenes in the book.

- Many of the topics covered in the *Picture Word Book* are classified by place. Help children find the same or similar places in their environments.

Using the *Picture Word Book* to play the games suggested below is a delightful way to discover the variety in the book.

- **I Spy:** As you enjoy the book together, take turns saying "I spy something red," or "I spy something round," or, "I spy something with four legs."

- Category Games such as **Twenty Questions:** Begin by saying: *I'm thinking of something that belongs in a house.* The child then asks questions about the object such as *Does it belong in a kitchen? Do you eat with it?* The questions can only be answered by the word *Yes* or *No.*

- **Word Hunt:** As children become interested in recognizing words, invite them on a Word Hunt. Give them lists of foods to look for that are pictured at the market, for example. See if they can find them in the *Picture Word Book*.

- **Collecting Words** Children may enjoy collecting their favorite words from the *Picture Word Book* and writing them on cards. Or, work with children to make your own picture word book together that has children's choices for the words to be included.

Let the *Macmillan/McGraw-Hill Picture Word Book* be a part of a home or a classroom writing center. Encourage children to use the book during quiet reading or journal writing times. Take it on class or family trips. As children begin to experiment with writing messages and making lists, they may naturally use the *Picture Word Book* for ideas. As they become interested in the spelling of words, encourage them to look to the *Picture Word Book* for help.

For some children, the *Picture Word Book* will be their first reading book. Help children discover a love for and appreciation of language through this introduction to printed words.

Contents

Fghijk

stUVwxy

top

bottom

on

off

up

down

out

in

IN THE PARK

grass

jungle gym

bench

slide

tunnel

tree

ountain

swings

merry-go-round

next to

in front of

behind

through

over

under

around

7

IN THE HOME

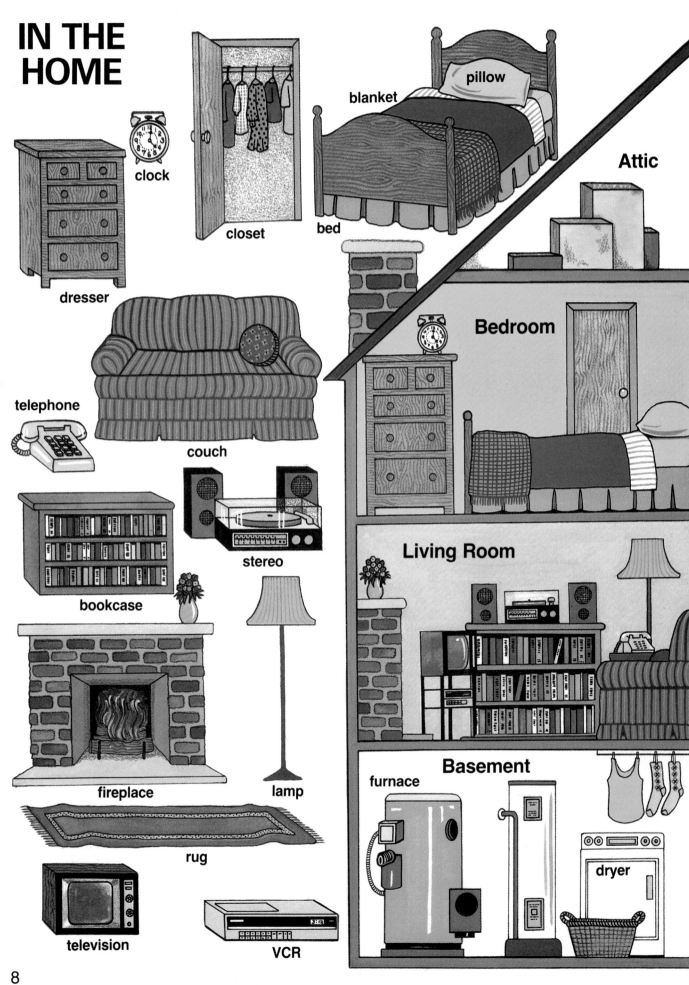

clock

closet

blanket

pillow

bed

Attic

dresser

telephone

couch

Bedroom

bookcase

stereo

Living Room

fireplace

lamp

Basement

furnace

rug

television

VCR

dryer

8

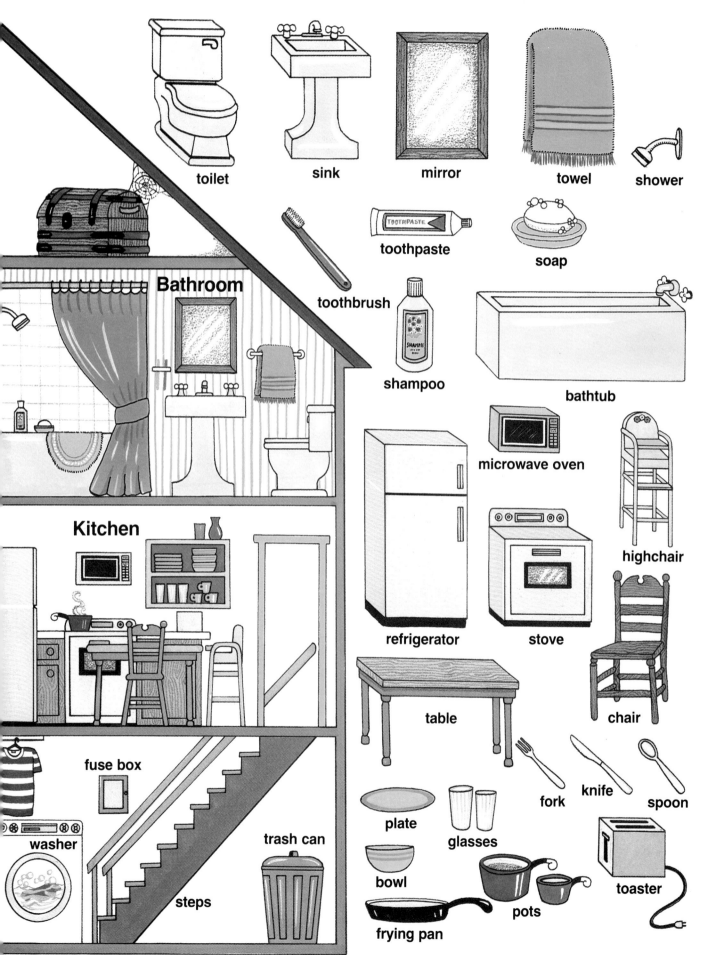

toilet

sink

mirror

towel

shower

toothpaste

soap

toothbrush

shampoo

bathtub

Bathroom

microwave oven

highchair

Kitchen

refrigerator

stove

chair

table

fork

knife

spoon

fuse box

plate

glasses

washer

trash can

bowl

toaster

steps

pots

frying pan

9

HOMES

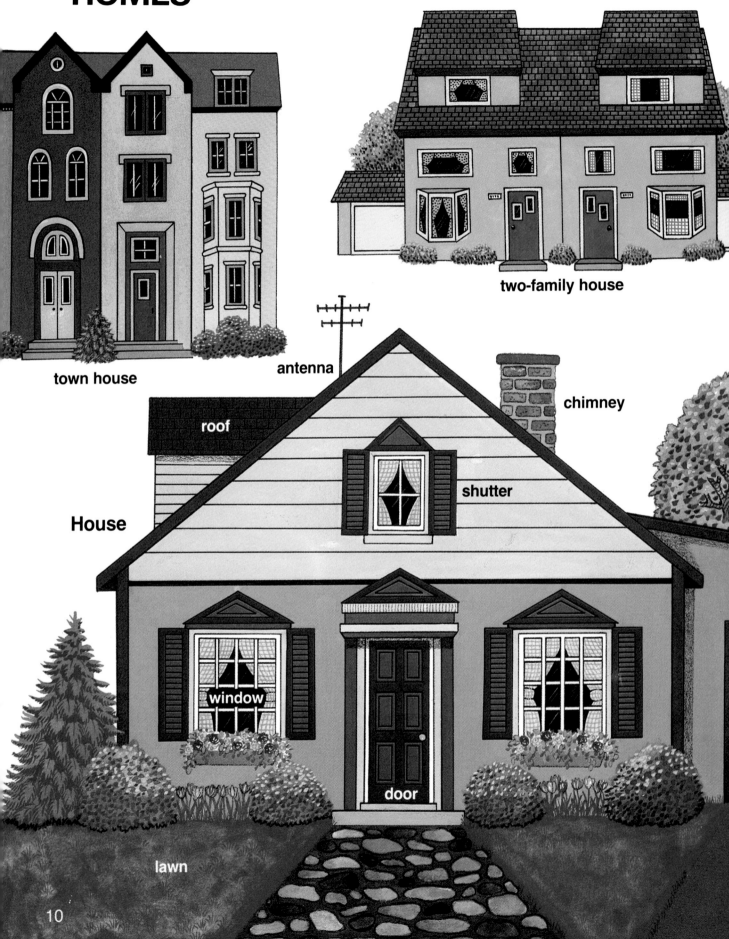

town house

two-family house

antenna

chimney

roof

shutter

House

window

door

lawn

mobile home

apartment building

log cabin

tepee

house on stilts

garage

adobe house

driveway

igloo

11

AT SCHOOL

globe

headphones

aquarium

tape

easel

paintbrush

tape recorder

paints

student

paper

scissors

markers

bulletin board

clock

flag

teacher

chalkboard

chalk

eraser

calendar

computer

book

table

chair

abacus

pencil sharpener

paste

crayons

pencil

9:00 Shared Reading
9:30 Journal Writing
10:00 Music
10:30 Recess
11:00 Individual Activities

OCTOBER

13

AT THE SUPERMARKET

bread

rice

cereal

chicken

meat

fish

spices

cheese

milk

apples

eggs

oranges

grapes

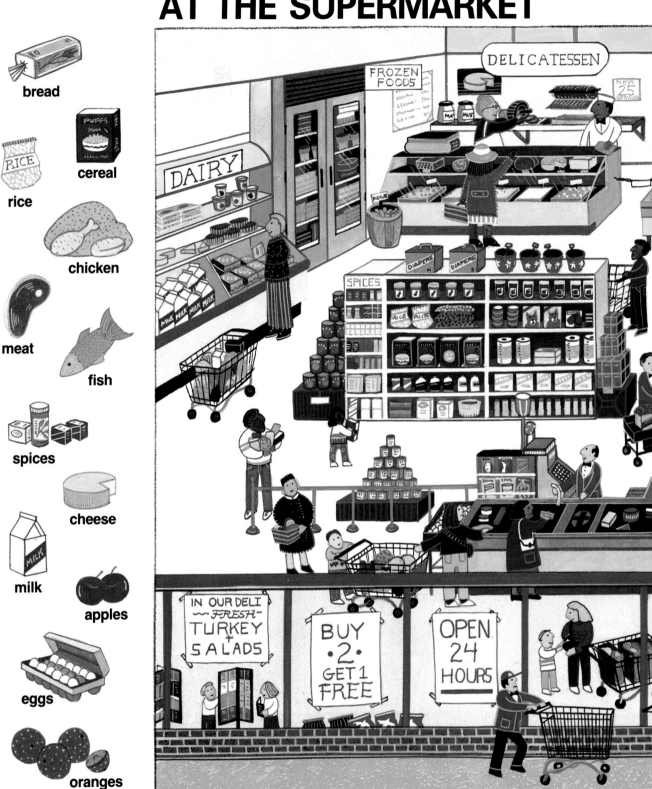

lemons

bananas

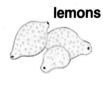

tomatoes

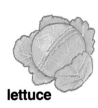

lettuce

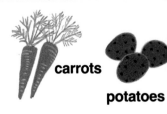

carrots

potatoes

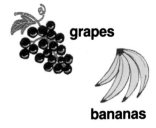

MEAT & POULTRY

BAKERY

FRUITS VEGETABLES

EMPLOYEES ONLY

SUPERMARKET

OUT   IN

RECYCLE CANS

UNA 5H
SALE
9¢ EACH

shopping cart

shopper

cash register

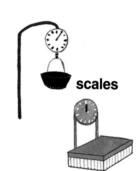

scales

clerk

checkout counter

canned food

paper towels

pet food

broccoli

corn

string beans

peanut butter

jelly

tissues

A FARM IN THE COUNTRY

dog

hay

hoe

pitchfork

pump

pail

pickup truck

weather vane

scarecrow

fence

plow

tractor

pigpen

porch

hayloft

chicken coop

garden

rooster

hen

chick

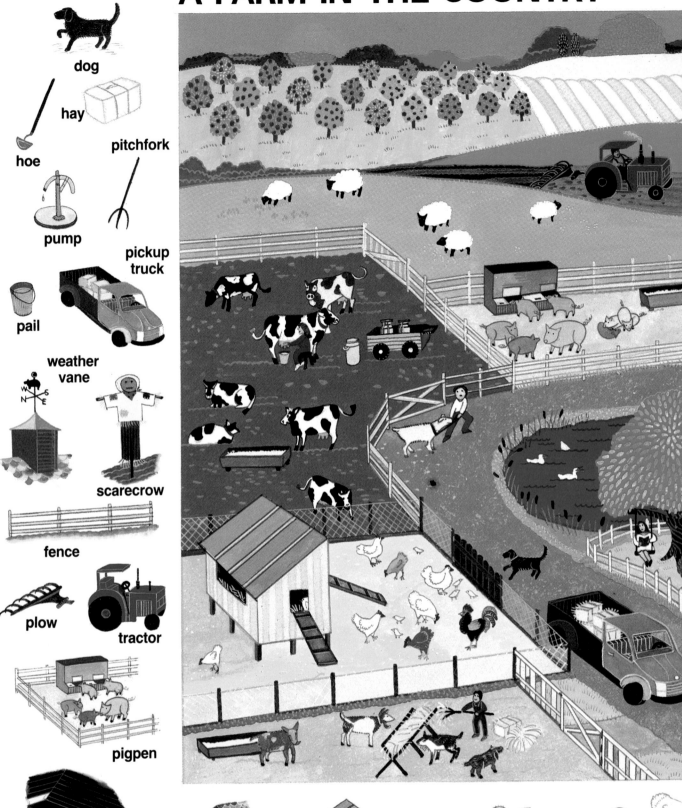

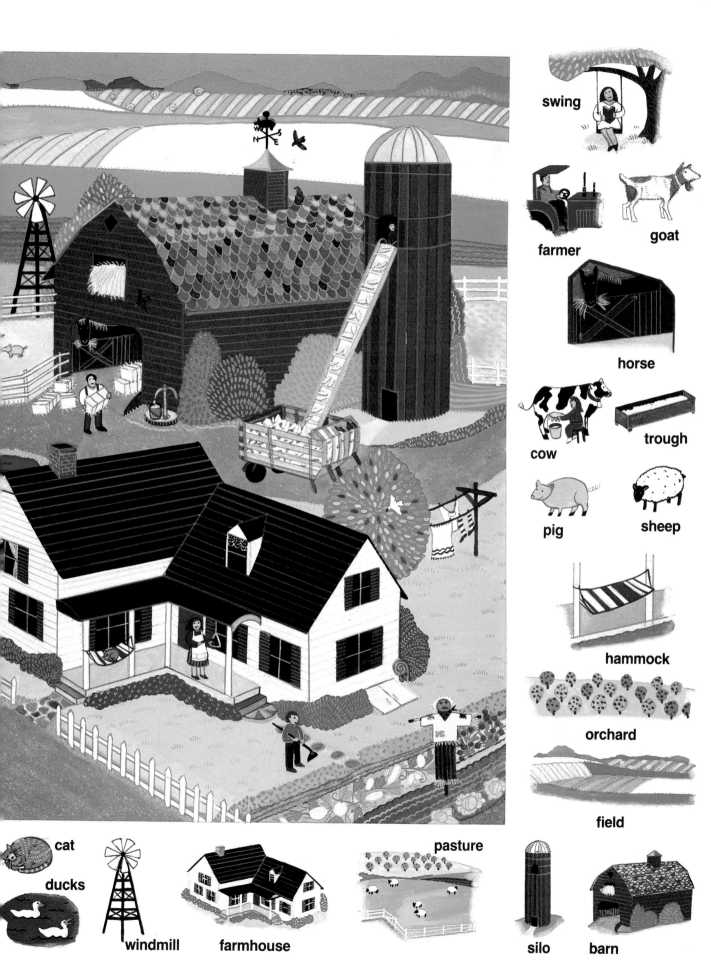

swing

farmer

goat

horse

cow

trough

pig

sheep

hammock

orchard

field

cat

ducks

windmill

farmhouse

pasture

silo

barn

17

IN THE CITY

restaurant and café

waiter

museum

fruit and vegetable stand

dry cleaner

newsstand

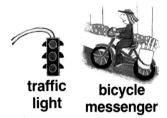
firehouse

traffic light

bicycle messenger

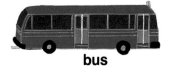
bus

coffee shop

mail carrier

hot dog stand

apartment building

bank

street light

school

subway

skyscraper

telephone booth

department store

police officer

taxicab

parking garage

bus stop

parking meter

church

post office

hospital

library

mailbox

bookstore

movie theater

fire hydrant

herd

gazelle

rhinoceros

ostrich

grasshopper

butterfly

flowers

hyena

leopard

vines

parrot

monkey

toucan

tiger

gorilla

ferns

JUNGLE

20

AFRICAN PLAIN

giraffes

secretary bird

hippopotamus

zebras

grass

vulture

jackal

lion

elephants

chimpanzee

boa constrictor

21

DESERT

cactus

mule deer

fox

roadrunner

coyote

burrow

jackrabbit

gila monster

rattlesnake

lizard

spider

mouse

scorpion

peak

valley

MOUNTAINS

eagle

bighorn
sheep

mountain
goats

waterfall

stream

mountain lion

bear

wildflowers

moss

cave

bats

23

leaves

acorns

raccoon

owl

oak tree

pine

FOREST

branch

pine cones

porcupine

woodpecker

birch

deer

moose

opossum

rabbit

trunk

violets

skunk

mushrooms

squirrel

chipmunk

caterpillar

SWAMP

cypress

mangrove

beaver

flamingos

alligator

cattails

dragonfly

egret

reeds

muskrat

water lilies

turtle

frog

POLAR REGIONS

musk ox

reindeer

walruses

ice and snow

ermine

snowy owl

arctic fox

polar bear

arctic hares

sea urchins

turtle

dolphin

sea horse

jellyfish

tuna

sky

penguins

flying fish

seals

ocean

crab

starfish

mussels

barnacles

sponges

sea anemone

seaweed

coral

lobster

octopus

swordfish

eel

manta ray

whale

UNDER THE SEA

27

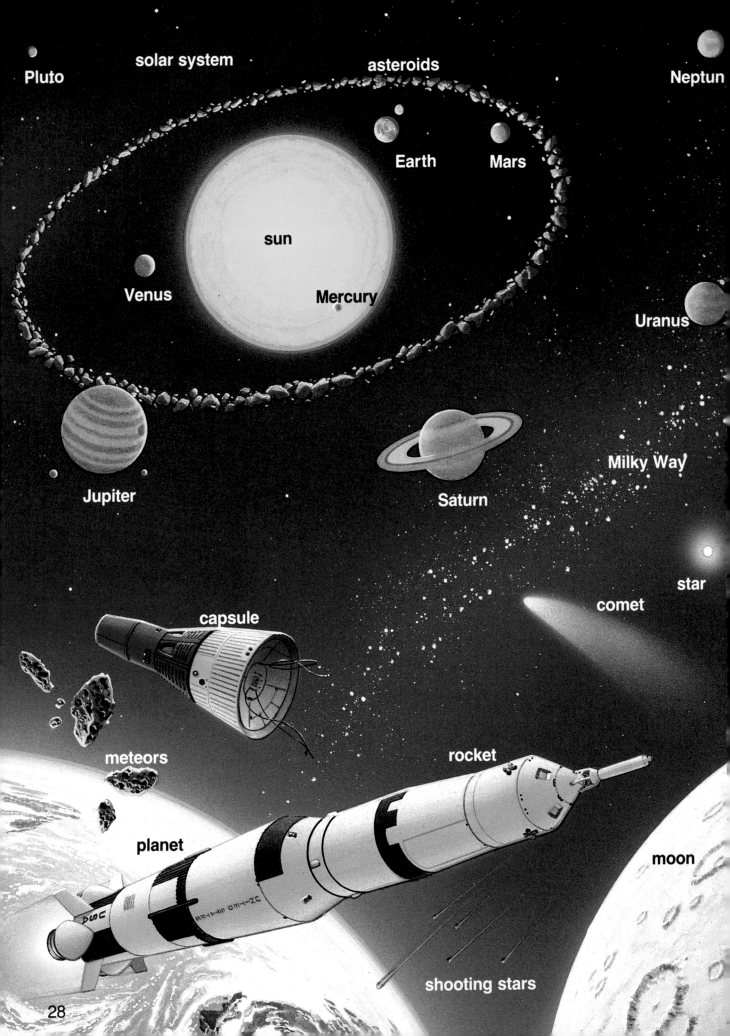

OUTER SPACE

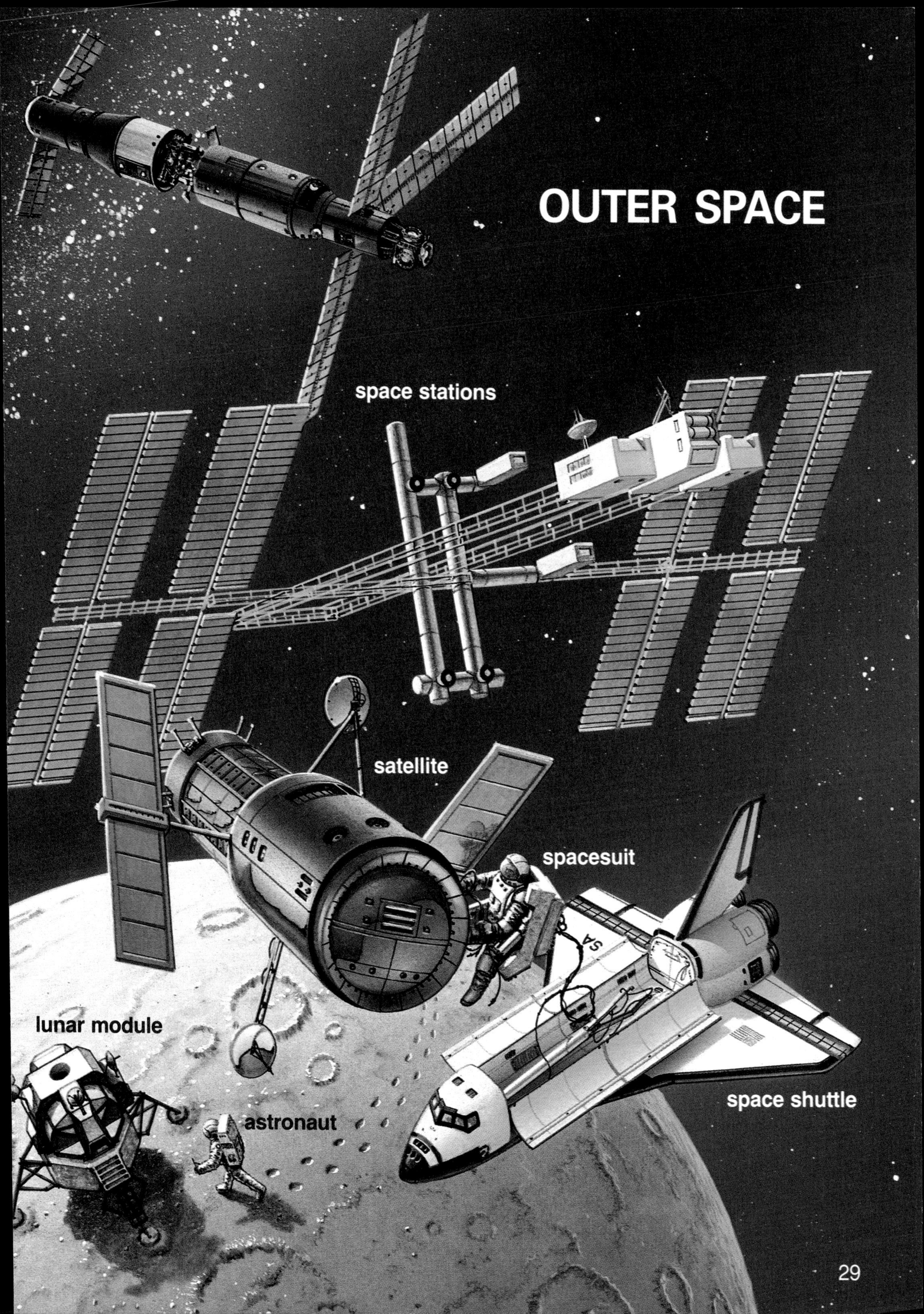

space stations

satellite

spacesuit

lunar module

astronaut

space shuttle

SPRING

flying a kite

hill

hiking

playing baseball

pond

ducks

fishing

mowing the grass

jogging

riding a bicycle

roller-skating

robin

buds

spring flowers

kite

baseball and glove

backpack

eggs

bird's nest

roller skates

bat

30

SUMMER

playing tennis

rowing a boat

watering the flowers

playing volleyball

swimming

net

inner tube

SWIM AREA

having a picnic

picnic basket

picnic table

jumping rope

climbing a tree

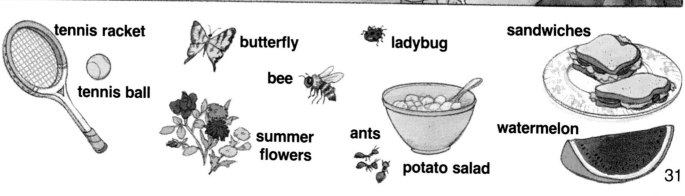

tennis racket

butterfly

ladybug

sandwiches

tennis ball

bee

summer flowers

ants

potato salad

watermelon

FALL

playing soccer

hay

going on a hayride

wagon

raking leaves

carving pumpkins

picking apples

ladder

apples

cider

pumpkin

basket

soccer ball

soccer shoes

geese

squirrel

acorns

rake

WINTER

skiing

sledding

holly bush

playing ice hockey

shoveling snow

ice

ice-skating

bird feeder

making a snowman

making snow angels

evergreen tree

making snowballs

sled

hockey stick

cardinal

icicles

ice skates

sparrows

ski poles

skis

hockey puck

holly leaves and berries

33

CLOTHES WE WEAR

A Rainy Day

cloud

umbrella

rain hat

rain

raincoat

poncho

rain boots

puddle

sun

lifeguard

sunglasses

T-shirt

sun hat

shorts

bathing suit

sneakers

sand

sandals

A Sunny Day

cap

jeans

dress

jacket

sweater

pajamas

pants

socks

snow

earmuffs

hat

scarf

mittens

gloves

snowsuit

snowman

parka

snow boots

A Snowy Day

skirt

nightgown

coat

sweatshirt

suspenders

shirt

sweatpants

slippers

shoes

AT THE AIRPORT

runway

cockpit

cabin

jet engine

Airplane

tail

wing

nose

baggage truck

NEWSSTAND

RESTAURA

GATE 5

flight attendants

gate

waiting area

check-in counter

boarding ramp

control tower

mechanic

baggage compartment

landing gear

pilot

passengers

observation area

FT SHOP

arrival and departure monitors

ticket agent

GATES 5-10

rest rooms

INFORMATION

ticket counter

information desk

baggage 275 carousel

security check

metal detector

arding pass

garment bag

carry-on luggage

skycap

baggage cart

suitcases

TRAINS

tunnel

tank car

steam locomotive

livestock car

switch tower

caboose

Rio Grande

4065

dining car

passenger car

diesel locomotive

railroad crossing

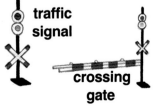

traffic signal

crossing gate

rail switch

bench

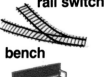

engineer

passengers

conductor

porter

trestle

refrigerator car

automobile car

·L·G·B· 4059

boxcar

flatcar

D&R&W 4060

2 G B

sleeping car

267

TRAIN STATION

TICKETS

MAP

TAXI

TAXI

TAXI

platform

stationmaster

train signal

waiting room

TICKETS

ticket window

ties

tracks

rails

TAXI

taxi station

AT THE HARBOR

tugboat

barge

flag

buoy

freighter

lifeboat

container truck

motorboat

oars

dock

rowboat

canoe

BOAT HOUSE

hull

outboard motor

submarine

smokestack

lighthouse

foghorn

bow

portholes

stern

ocean liner

pier

mast

sail

fishing boat

anchor

sailboat

ferry

passengers

·BLUE FERRY·

sea gull

gas pump

GOING PLACES

trailer truck

PAY TOLL 1 MILE

SPEED LIMIT 30

car

bus

school bus

ONE WAY

STOP

SCHOOL CROSSING

NO PARKING

fire engine

DO NOT ENTER

jeep

NO U TURN

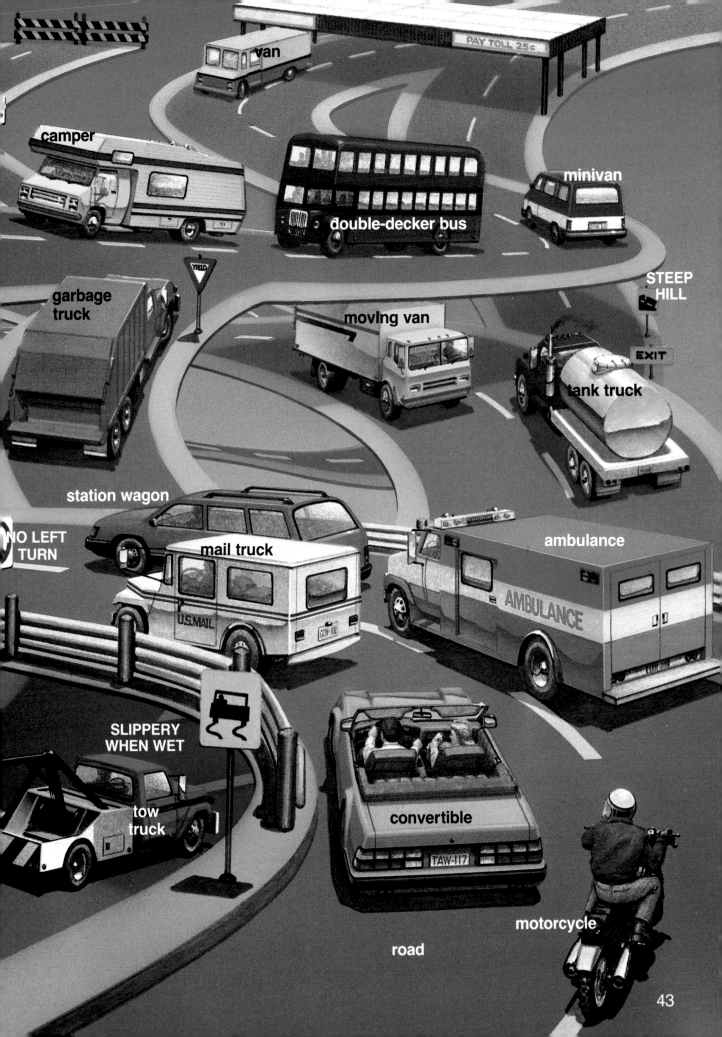

van

PAY TOLL 25¢

camper

double-decker bus

minivan

garbage truck

YIELD

moving van

STEEP HILL

EXIT

tank truck

station wagon

NO LEFT TURN

mail truck

U.S. MAIL

ambulance

AMBULANCE

SLIPPERY WHEN WET

tow truck

convertible

TAW-117

motorcycle

road

43

beam

crane

girder

scaffold

ladder

lumber

forklift

electrical cables

jackhammer

hand truck

44

power shovel

dumptruck

bulldozer

cement mixer

cement

worker

steamroller

hard hat

shovel

goggles

blowtorch

wheelbarrow

welder

pipes

lunch box

saw

wrenches

sledgehammer

vise

sawhorse

hacksaw

coping saw

try square

level

hammer

masking tap

safety knife

hand drill

staple

tool box

46

WORKING WITH TOOLS

paint brush

jigsaw

paint tray

electric drill

paint roller

drill press

drill bits

clamps

tape measure

screwdrivers

pliers

wire cutters

ruler

plane

circular saw

paint

glue

screws

bolts

nuts

nails

file

drop cloth

sandpaper

47

MAKING MUSIC

harp

triangle

Chorus

piano

sheet music

singer

bagpipe

tambourine

maracas

trombone

harmonica

guitar

saxophone

xylophone

Orchestra

clarinet

tuba

cymbals

French horn

baton

oboe

bass

violin

trumpet

flute

conductor

music stand

cello

bugle

recorder

piccolo

accordion

drum

A FAMILY ALBUM

me

my mother and father

my sister and broth

my mother and her
parents

my grandmother and grandfather and me

my mother and her
brother

my uncle and me

my dog Winky

my father and his sister

my aunt, her daughter and son, and their stepfather

my parents and their niece and nephew

my cousins and me

all of us ♡

VISITING THE DOCTOR

doctor

stethoscope

scale

cotton balls

gauze pads

tongue depressors

bandages

bulb syringe

tweezers

thermometer

blood pressure cuff

nurse

doctor's bag

patient

examining table

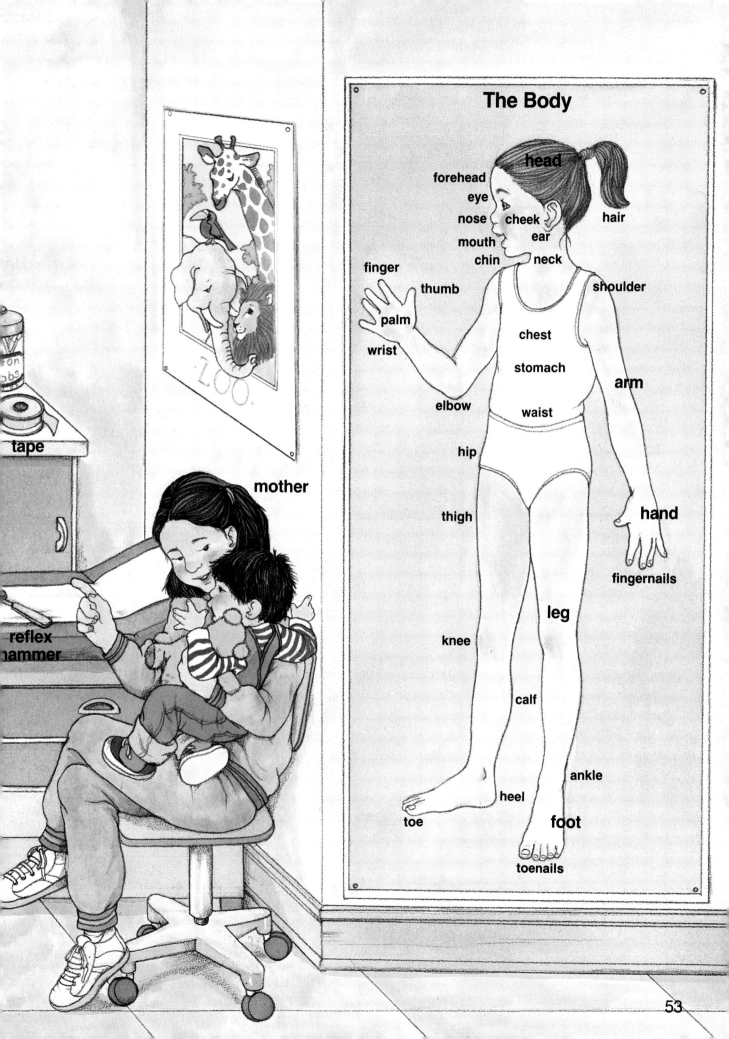

tape

mother

reflex
hammer

The Body

head

forehead

eye

nose · cheek

mouth · ear

chin · neck

hair

finger

thumb

shoulder

palm

wrist

chest

stomach

arm

waist

elbow

hip

thigh

hand

fingernails

leg

knee

calf

ankle

heel

toe · foot

toenails

THE WORLD OF FANTASY

castle

moat

drawbridge

sword

armor

shield

knight

giant

prince

princess

enchanted forest

unicorn

troll

elf

wand

fairy godmother

fairy

dungeon

dwarf

dragon

treasure

flags

crow's nest

sails

pirate ship

magic carpet

genie

crown

king

queen

staff

wizard

lamp

55

NUMBERS, OPPOSITES, AND SHAPES

1 one

2 two

3 three

4 four

5 five

6 six

7 seven

8 eight

9 nine

10 ten

many

tall

short

few

high

low

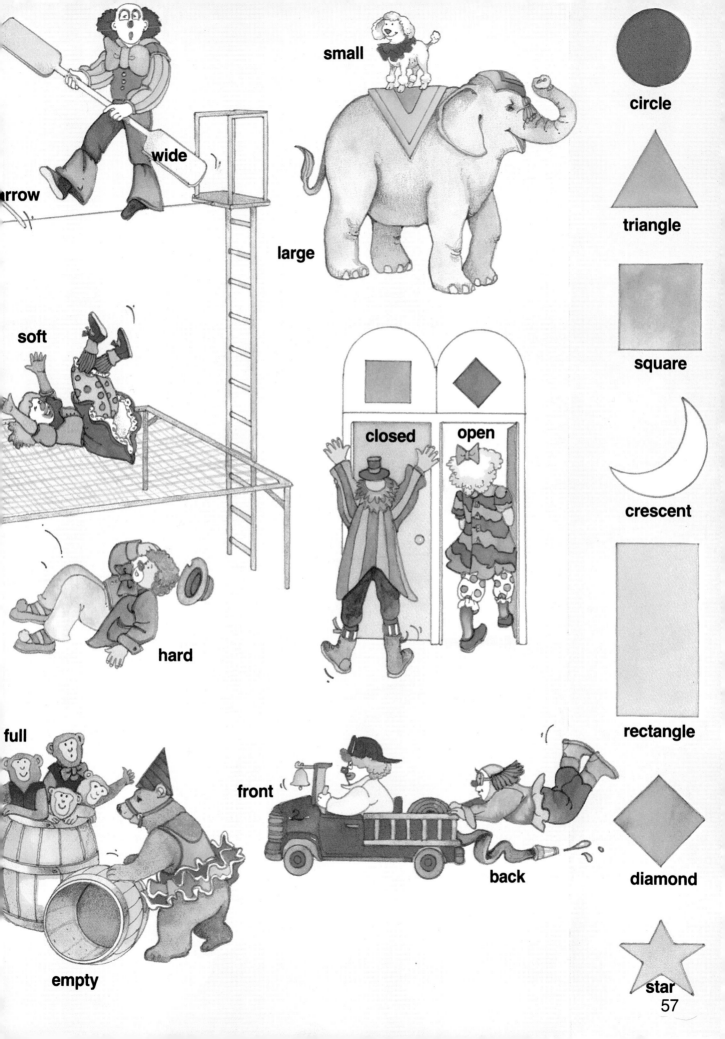

narrow

wide

small

large

soft

hard

full

empty

closed

open

front

back

circle

triangle

square

crescent

rectangle

diamond

star

57

THE ALPHABET AND COLORS

Aa Bb

white

Cc Dd Ee Ff

pink

Gg Hh Ii Jj Kk

red

Ll Mm Nn Oo

orange

Pp Qq Rr Ss

Tt Uu Vv Ww

yellow

Xx Yy Zz

green   blue   purple   brown   gray   blac

WORD LIST